W0081736

Outside In and the Inside Out

story and pictures
by Emmy Kastner

a story about Arnold Lobel

VIKING

 **his story begins** with a boy and a pair of wet socks.

Since this is a book about a man named Arnold Lobel, who wrote and illustrated books for kids, you may have expected the story to begin with something like "Arnold Lobel was born on May 22, 1933."

But lots of stories start that way.

We all know what it feels like to have wet socks. So we'll start there.

Maybe he had been in a water balloon fight

with an octopus.

Perhaps Arnold had been playing in the rain?

No, it was actually the snow.

Arnold had wet socks.

And maybe it was his grandma  who thought

that wet socks led to the sneezes

that led to the fever  that led to bed rest.

However it happened, Arnold was sick.

He spent months in the hospital

drawing  and reading

and drawing some more

while he recovered, watching the outside

from the inside.

Eventually, Arnold was better.

He was good at telling stories
and discovered worlds at
the tip of his pencil.

His classmates were enthralled . . .

. . . until they weren't.

Arnold retreated, keeping his impressive stories to himself. For a long while, he remained a bit of an outsider, which was often hard on the inside.

But Arnold enjoyed being a quiet observer.

He listened.
He watched everything.
And Arnold read a lot.

It was a downhill sprint to the library.
Then back home, uphill, with five new
books that were his for two weeks.

What were his favorite stories?
The ones that made him laugh!

The rhymes! The illustrations! The foolishness!
Arnold was inspired.

He embraced the absurd
off the page as well.

As a young boy, Arnold tried
to adopt a lobster he found in
the family fridge in an effort
to save its life.

As a grown man, he kept a
gorilla suit in his closet,
though he rarely found
the right occasion to wear it.

There was a plastic goose named Gladys
in his living room. It even lit up!

Now, why have a pet lobster,
a gorilla suit,
or an illuminated plastic goose
beside your favorite chair?
Arnold may have answered, *"Why not?"*

While he loved the silly and absurd, he was
serious about what he wanted to do . . .

Arnold was a young man

who wanted to make art.

So he packed his bags

and went to art school.

He painted  and

drew  and painted

until his arm nearly fell off.

There, he directed a play

and met a woman.

Anita loved the theater, and was an artist, too.

They fell in love,  got married,

and built a life together.

Arnold got a job and worked

and worked  and worked.

But the buttoned-up business world
was not a fit for Arnold.

With brushes, his paints, and a pen,
Arnold Lobel set out to find his way
as a professional daydreamer.

Arnold got his start in the book world illustrating
other people's manuscripts.

Early on, there were salmon. Sixty-four pages
of salmon, to be exact. (That's a lot of fish!)

And books about microscopes, Jewish holidays,
caterpillars, turtles, quarreling friends, tigers, and flutes.

From his first book to his last, and on the pages
of close to one hundred books in between,
Arnold experimented with style.

After all, there are many ways
to draw a tree.

Mouse Tales

Arnold Lobel was an artist who
put himself into his work.
Literally.

You'll find him, and his mustache,
right there in the illustrations.

PIGERICKS

You'll also find his turtle, Wilbira,
on the pages. And his cats, Orson
and Alfred, too.
A clay pot, maybe even his lamp,
a favorite chair, the roses outside
his window . . .

His outside, in.

Now, making the art came easy for Arnold.
But finding the words to tell his own stories?
That was intimidating.

Chewing pencils in cozy corners,
Arnold found his words to share.

Sometimes they were big.

He trusted young readers with bold,
beautiful words.

Sometimes he handed the words over
for his wife, Anita, to illustrate.

creakingoverflowedsomersaultedlistening intimidating humming cozy for glorious mountains fountains bumping wizard blinding slouched perfect surprised porcupines royal kingdoms screeching acc beautifully yellow humming seashore downstairs perhaps for

VEXATiOUS

AVALANCHE

PREDICAMENT

decorate

And sometimes he made the words rhyme.
Arnold loved crafting clever design.
It was a wonderful game
with those tricky restraints.
And the results? Always sublime!

Before the words come together,
every story starts with an idea.
And every idea comes
from somewhere.

Arnold's most famous books got their start in a Vermont swamp on a summer vacation with his family.

He noticed the way frogs seemed to smile, as if caught in a pleasant daydream. So green. So shiny. So beautiful. And those slow-moving toads, quite introverted and dyspeptic. (Yes, grab a dictionary for that one!)

There was a story there somewhere . . .

Years later, Arnold gave Frog and Toad the stories
from his own life.
He was a very good friend.
He knew what it meant to be generous,
to be lonely,
to worry,
to be thankful,
to celebrate . . .
and how difficult it was to eat just *one* cookie.

Arnold Lobel tenderly put his entire being
into the friendship of a frog and a toad.

His inside, out.

The stories were written, then came the sketches.

On one particularly ordinary day,
which may have felt a lot like today,
it all came together. There they were.

Frog and Toad found their way in the world.
Readers fell in love with them,
and the books won big awards.

What makes these four books so special?
That's for you to decide.

But maybe, we're all a little bit Frog.
And we're all a little bit Toad.
Arnold Lobel understood that very well.

He was honest with his readers, and isn't that what
we all want? Someone to tell us the truth, even in a
made-up world where a frog and a toad are friends
who drink tea, wear bathing suits, and get their
mail delivered by a snail?

It's nice to see the books you've made
in a bookstore or the library.

It's nice to know your books are treasured
in schools and in homes on bookshelves.

It's especially nice to buy some new
art supplies, and to make
even more books.

And that's exactly what Arnold Lobel did.

In his books,
the inside came out
and the outside came in.

A man letting the indoors outside
to see the world.

An owl letting the wind inside.

And in his life,
the inside came out
and the outside came in as well.

A man who loved his family bravely let them know
there was more love for him to find.

A new world with a new love.

But there is comfort in knowing, even for Arnold, that
a man who put himself into the books he made is never
completely gone.

Every story comes to an end.
Arnold became very sick—
the sort of ending that came far too soon.

Rather than let the sadness take over completely,
he decided to see things from a different perspective.

In *The Turnaround Wind*, you can turn the page around to see a whole new illustration, another side of the same story.

Though every ending is a new beginning, it doesn't make goodbyes easy.

He spent the last year of his life doing what he loved, making his very last book in a very clever way.

Whether they're tales of
a frog and a toad,
an unruly boy who turns into a dragon,
a wizard who paints a town blue,
an owl,
a cloud,
a grasshopper,
a witch,
a pig,
or that mouse with a mustache
telling tales to his kids tucked into bed . . .

we'll find Arnold in his stories.
And we can find ourselves there, too.

KISS ME
IT'S
MORNING

We close the books and know
that everything, from the ordinary
to the extraordinary, is special—
whether we are on
the inside or the outside.

Thank you for the stories, Arnold.
We are very pleased to have them.

904

Dear Reader,

I carried *Frog and Toad Are Friends* in my backpack in second grade. I had gym shoes, my lunch, and that book. I was the new kid that year. We moved into the middle of the woods in a small town in Michigan. I would go out by a creek, bringing along little chairs and mugs for the frogs (or maybe they were toads?) that I'd borrowed from the My Little Pony Palace. I was certain *some* amphibian would join me, likely wearing a jacket missing a button. It felt possible they'd take a seat and pick up a cup of tea. Arnold Lobel made things up and I truly believed them. I still do.

This would be a good spot in this letter to make a confession: I didn't want to make this book. I was wildly intimidated by the thought of telling Arnold Lobel's life story. It seemed impossible to make a book about someone I admire so deeply. I spent a lot of years waiting for a frog to show up. And one cold October day, as I was watching my daughter play tennis at the YMCA, I set down the biography of Lobel I was reading and briefly closed my eyes. I thought, *Arnold, am I going to make a book about you?* I wasn't trying to actually ask his spirit. Maybe I was asking myself? Either way, that very instant, a woman sitting near me hit my knee and shouted, "Frog!" I opened my eyes, completely confused as to how she was reading my mind. I saw her pointing to the *actual* frog who was hopping toward me and then stopped at my feet! A *frog*? On the *indoor tennis court*? *On a cold October day*? That's the moment I gave up trying to fight myself from making this book and knew that I was meant to pursue it. What a tremendous honor it has been to dive into Arnold Lobel's life and work. I am forever changed as an artist. (And I even have my own Gladys the Goose lighting up my studio now!)

Born in Los Angeles, Arnold Lobel moved to Schenectady, New York, with his parents when he was a baby. He'd grow up there with his mother and grandmother. This story starts with the wet socks that were the catalyst for two poignant parts of Arnold's life. First of all, they set off a domino effect of worsening tragedies: wet socks from playing in the snow led to a cold that led to an ear infection, followed by surgery for mastoiditis. Six months in the hospital, then six months at home recovering. He missed the entire second grade. Though the silver lining was that he spent the year drawing a lot. Whenever you do something every day, you get very good at it. Though a skillful young artist, he returned to third grade as an outsider. Stories helped him find his way back in. Arnold would reflect on how essential it was in his career to tap into that third-grade storyteller. So truly, those wet socks were also the catalyst for Lobel's finest storytelling as an adult, too.

Arnold moved to Brooklyn to attend Pratt University, earning his degree in illustration in 1955. After graduation, he and Anita, a fellow artist at Pratt, were married. Their family was growing with two kids, Adrianne and Adam, and he needed to find work. Arnold gave the world of advertising a go, working for a few agencies. The business world lacked the creative excitement he was drawn to. That's when a school of salmon would launch Arnold's prolific career. He got his foot in the door by illustrating *Red Tag Comes Back* for Harper & Row. His art consisted of watercolor, ink, and graphite. Though his style is always recognizable, it evolved in execution throughout his career—tight pen and ink, color separations, full paintings, watercolor with loose graphite lines. In his short life, he would illustrate nearly one hundred books. He called himself an "old workhorse" when he accepted his Caldecott Medal for *Fables* in 1981. He also won two Caldecott Honors—for *Frog and Toad Are Friends* (1971) and *Hildilid's Night* (1972). Arnold Lobel was a confident artist and a superstitious writer. With the help of his "writing chair and a special writing notebook and a writing ballpoint pen," he won the highest honor for writing in children's books, the Newbery Medal, in 1973 for *Frog and Toad Together*. Some of the books that he wrote were illustrated by his wife, Anita Lobel: *How the Rooster Saved the Day*, *A Treeful of Pigs*, *The Rose in My Garden*, and *On Market Street* (she won a Caldecott Honor for that book in 1982). The stories he told had a particular meter, pace, and rhythm. He wasn't in a hurry to tell a story. Not to say there weren't laughs and even wild ac-

tion, of course. He loved to laugh and to rhyme. He loved the absurd and embraced childlike wonderment through and through, inside out. He really did have a gorilla suit that his daughter made for him, fulfilling a lifelong dream to own one. He wore it on a few occasions while walking around his Brooklyn neighborhood.

As he found his way through life, stories and art were always with him. Themes of the outside and the inside are reflected in the pages of his books. Lobel was drawn to home (the inside) and nature (the outside). And sometimes those things were at odds with each other. The wind was coming inside, and chairs and lamps were sent outside to see the world. The vast majority of his characters are animals not only because that's what he loved to draw, but also because he felt they were easy for all his readers to connect with. He understood the silliness that sits squarely beside the tough stuff in life that we've all got to navigate—that's what it is to be human, even for a toad in a bathing suit. Or a book about the wind that is so powerful that the book literally spins around and around throughout the story. Arnold spent the last year of his life working on that book, *The Turnaround Wind*. In the eulogy published in *The Horn Book*, James Marshall,

Arnold's friend and fellow author/illustrator, discussed Arnold's approach to death. "He said he'd decided to approach it as his new job, something that he had to do as well as he could." Arnold did just that. He told his story in the way he best could: in a picture book. He used the tender parts of his own life to create a powerful allegory of the AIDS epidemic that was turning the world upside down, all while he battled the disease himself. Surrounded by the love of his friends; family; and his partner, Howard Weiner, Arnold remained a storyteller until his very end.

My hope is that every page of this book is both reverential and referential. Let me explain. To be *reverential* is to be respectful, appreciative, and admiring. I adore Arnold Lobel's work and am moved by who he was as a person. And to be *referential*, that means to make a reference to something. In this case, the text and illustrations on every page are filled with easter eggs from his books. Have fun looking for them!

I'll end my note to you with something that rings loudly in my ears as I reflect on who Arnold Lobel was: Let us be true to ourselves and one another, both in our lives and on the page. At the end of his life, Lobel told his friends and his family "that if they wish to do something nice for me, ask them to look at the books. Because that's where they'll find me." I'm grateful we've got so many places to find him.

Yours in admiration,

Emmy Kastner

Sources

Berry, John F. "The Lobels: A Marriage of Two Drawing Boards." *The Washington Post*, 13 June 1982. washingtonpost.com/archive/entertainment/books/1982/06/13/the-lobels-a-marriage-of-two-drawing-boards/ff29318e-73b0-4169-b5fd-662be645d94c.

Free Library Rare Book Department. "Arnold Lobel (1973)—Profiles in Literature No. 15." YouTube, March 20, 2023. Accessed October 9, 2024. youtube.com/watch?v=-ewz8q7laCo.

Lobel, Arnold. "1981 Caldecott Medal Acceptance Speech." American Library Association, 1981. Recording. Arnold Lobel_Caldecott_Fables_1981.mp3.

Marshall, James. "Arnold Lobel." *The Horn Book Magazine.* May 1, 1988. hbook.com/story/arnold-lobel.

McCullough, David W. "Arnold Lobel and Friends." *The New York Times*, November 11, 1979. nytimes.com/1979/11/11/archives/arnold-lobel-and-friends-lobel.html.

Natov, Roni, and Geraldine Deluca. "An Interview with Arnold Lobel." *The Lion and the Unicorn*, vol. 1, no. 1 (1977): 72–96. doi.org/10.1353/uni.0.0119.

Rollin, Lucy. "The Astonished Witness Disclosed: An Interview with Arnold Lobel." *Children's Literature in Education*, vol. 15, no. 4 (December 1984): 191–197. doi.org/10.1007/bf01137182.

Shannon, George. *Arnold Lobel.* Twayne Pub, 1989.

Lobel Bibliography

Books Written and Illustrated by Arnold Lobel (unless otherwise noted)

A Zoo for Mister Muster (1962)

A Holiday for Mister Muster (1963)

Prince Bertram the Bad (1963)

Giant John (1964)

Lucille (1964)

The Bears of the Air (1965)

Martha the Movie Mouse (1966)

The Comic Adventures of Old Mother Hubbard and Her Dog (1968)

The Great Blueness and Other Predicaments (1968)

Small Pig (1969)

Frog and Toad Are Friends (1970)

Ice-Cream Cone Coot, and Other Rare Birds (1971)

On the Day Peter Stuyvesant Sailed into Town (1971)

Frog and Toad Together (1972)

Mouse Tales (1972)

The Man Who Took the Indoors Out (1974)

Owl at Home (1975)

Frog and Toad All Year (1976)

How the Rooster Saved the Day, illustrated by Anita Lobel (1977)

Mouse Soup (1977)

Grasshopper on the Road (1978)

Days with Frog and Toad (1979)

A Treeful of Pigs, illustrated by Anita Lobel (1979)

Fables (1980)

Uncle Elephant (1981)

On Market Street, illustrated by Anita Lobel (1981)

Ming Lo Moves the Mountain (1982)

The Book of Pigericks: Pig Limericks (1983)

The Rose in My Garden, illustrated by Anita Lobel (1984)

Whiskers & Rhymes (1985)

The Turnaround Wind (1988)

Odd Owls & Stout Pigs: A Book of Nonsense, color by Adrianne Lobel (2009)

The Frogs and Toads All Sang, color by Adrianne Lobel (2009)

Books Illustrated by Arnold Lobel

Happy Times with Holiday Rhymes by Tamar Grand (1958)

My First Book of Prayers by Edythe Scharfstein and Sol Scharfstein, also illustrated by Ezekiel Schloss (1958)

All About Jewish Holidays and Customs by Morris Epstein (1959)

The Book of Chanukah: Poems, Riddles, Stories, Songs and Things to Do by Edythe Scharfstein and Sol Scharfstein, also illustrated by Ezekiel Schloss (1959)

The Complete Book of Hanukkah by Kinneret Chiel (1959)

Holidays Are Nice: Around the Year with the Jewish Child by Robert Garvey, also illustrated by Ezekiel Schloss (1960)

Red Tag Comes Back by Fred Phleger (1961)

Something Old, Something New by Susan Rhinehart (1961)

Little Runner of the Longhouse by Betty Baker (1962)

Let's Be Indians by Peggy Parish (1962)

The Secret Three by Mildred Myrick (1963)

Greg's Microscope by Millicent E. Selsam (1963)

Terry and the Caterpillars by Millicent E. Selsam (1963)

The Quarreling Book by Charlotte Zolotow (1963)

Miss Suzy by Miriam Young (1964)

Red Fox and His Canoe by Nathaniel Benchley (1964)

Dudley Pippin by Phil Ressner (1965)

Let's Get Turtles by Millicent E. Selsam (1965)

The Magic Spectacles and Other Easy-to-Read Stories by Lilian Moore (1965)

Someday by Charlotte Zolotow (1965)

The Witch on the Corner by Felice Holman (1966)

Oscar Otter by Nathaniel Benchley (1966)

Benny's Animals and How He Put Them in Order by Millicent E. Selsam (1966)

The Strange Disappearance of Arthur Cluck by Nathaniel Benchley (1967)

Let's Be Early Settlers with Daniel Boone by Peggy Parish (1967)

The Star Thief by Andrea DiNoto (1968)

Ants Are Fun by Mildred Myrick (1968)

The Four Little Children Who Went Around the World by Edward Lear (1968)

I'll Fix Anthony by Judith Viorst (1969)

Sam the Minuteman by Nathaniel Benchley (1969)

Junk Day on Juniper Street and Other Easy-to-Read Stories by Lilian Moore (1967)

The Terrible Tiger by Jack Prelutsky (1970)

The New Vestments by Edward Lear (1970)

Hansel and Gretel by the Brothers Grimm (1971)

The Master of Miracle: A New Novel of the Golem by Sulamith Ish-Kishor (1971)

Miss Suzy's Easter Surprise by Miriam Young (1972)

Seahorse by Robert A. Morris (1972)

Tot Botot and His Little Flute by Laura Cathon (1972)

As I Was Crossing Boston Common by Norma Farber (1973)

Good Ethan by Paula Fox (1973)

The Clay Pot Boy by Cynthia Jameson (1974)

Miss Suzy's Birthday by Miriam Young (1974)

Circus by Jack Prelutsky (1974)

Dinosaur Time by Peggy Parish (1974)

Nightmares: Poems to Trouble Your Sleep by Jack Prelutsky (1976)

Merry Merry Fibruary by Doris Orgel (1977)

Gregory Griggs and Other Nursery Rhyme People (1978)

Right as Right Can Be by Anne Rose (1978)

The Mean Old Mean Hyena by Jack Prelutsky (1978)

Tales of Oliver Pig by Jean van Leeuwen (1979)

The Headless Horseman Rides Tonight: More Poems to Trouble Your Sleep by Jack Prelutsky (1980)

The Tale of Meshka the Kvetch by Carol Chapman (1980)

More Tales of Oliver Pig by Jean van Leeuwen (1981)

The Random House Book of Poetry for Children by Jack Prelutsky (1983)

The Microscope by Maxine Kumin (1984)

A Three Hat Day by Laura Geringer (1985)

The Random House Book of Mother Goose (1986)

Hildilid's Night by Cheli Durán Ryan (1986)

Bear Gets Dressed by Harriet Ziefert (1986)

Bear's Busy Morning by Harriet Ziefert (1986)

Bear Goes Shopping by Harriet Ziefert (1986)

Bear All Year by Harriet Ziefert (1986)

Where's the Turtle? by Harriet Ziefert (1987)

Where's the Cat? by Harriet Ziefert (1987)

Where's the Dog? by Harriet Ziefert (1987)

Where's the Guinea Pig? by Harriet Ziefert (1987)

The Devil and Mother Crump by Valerie Scho Carey (1987)

Sing a Song of Popcorn: Every Child's Book of Poems by Beatrice Schenk de Regniers (1988)

Tyrannosaurus Was a Beast: Dinosaur Poems by Jack Prelutsky (1988)

For Arnold and the frog on the tennis court —E. K.

Special thanks to Dan Kastner, Linnaea and John Thomas, Hannah Mann,
the Kerlan Collection/University of Minnesota, Andrea Vernola, George Shannon,
Kate Renner, and Tamar Brazis.

VIKING
An imprint of Penguin Random House LLC
1745 Broadway, New York, New York 10019

First published in the United States of America by Viking, an imprint of Penguin Random House LLC, 2025

Copyright © 2025 by Emmy Kastner

Penguin Random House values and supports copyright. Copyright fuels creativity, encourages diverse voices,
promotes free speech, and creates a vibrant culture. Thank you for buying an authorized edition of this book
and for complying with copyright laws by not reproducing, scanning, or distributing any part of it in any form
without permission. You are supporting writers and allowing Penguin Random House to continue to publish
books for every reader. Please note that no part of this book may be used or reproduced in any manner for the
purpose of training artificial intelligence technologies or systems.

Viking & colophon are registered trademarks of Penguin Random House LLC.
The Penguin colophon is a registered trademark of Penguin Books Limited.

Visit us online at PenguinRandomHouse.com.

Library of Congress Cataloging-in-Publication Data is available.

ISBN 9780593692509

1 3 5 7 9 10 8 6 4 2

Manufactured in China
TOPL

Edited by Tamar Brazis   Design by Kate Renner   Text set in Bogue Slab

The art was made with acrylic gouache, pencil, and ink.
No artificial intelligence was used in the creation of art in this book.

The publisher does not have any control over and does not assume any responsibility
for author or third-party websites or their content.

The authorized representative in the EU for product safety and compliance is Penguin Random House Ireland,
Morrison Chambers, 32 Nassau Street, Dublin D02 YH68, Ireland, https://eu-contact.penguin.ie.

2 04